Also available in this series from Quadrille:

the little book of
JOY

Hardie Grant

QUADRILLE

Joy

Definition:
noun

A feeling of great pleasure
and happiness.

Jolly

Old

You

"Doing good to others is not a duty. It is a joy, for it increases your own health and happiness."

ZOROASTER

What are you doing today to bring yourself joy?

What are you doing today to bring joy to another?

What are you doing today to share your joy with others?

Joy does not demand anything of us. Joy does not only appear when we eventually have enough money or finally find the perfect partner. Joy is not waiting for our lives to fall into place before it makes itself felt. Joy is a constant companion made up of small moments.

It takes little more than a turn of the head to see joy. . .

In the eyelashes of your sleeping child.

Along the warm chest of your lover.

In the belly laugh of your oldest friend.

The inherently human sensation of euphoric joy is shared across the globe, and we have created the most glorious words to describe the physical and metaphysical expression of joy.

- **Mbuki-mvuki** (Swahili)
  verb
  To remove your clothes and dance wild and uninhibited.

- **Gigil** (Tagalog)
  noun
  The irresistible urge to pinch/squeeze someone you love or cherish, because they're just so cute.

- **Jouissance** (French)

  noun

  Physical or intellectual pleasure or delight.

- **Uňuhňat** (Czech)

  noun

  The desire to smother or crush by cuddling or fondling; to shower somebody with boundless love.

- **Ânanda** (Sanskrit)

  noun

  Bliss, lasting contentment; spiritual, 'unconditional' happiness.

"*If the sight of the blue skies fills you with joy, if a blade of grass springing up in the fields has power to move you, if the simple things of nature have a message that you understand, rejoice, for your soul is alive.*"

ELEONORA DUSE

The joy of saying. . .

"Why not?"

"Yes, I'd love to join you."

"Let's have all three courses."

"This is my treat."

"Now? Why not? Let's go."

Joy is found in the spiritual connection formed with other people, where the space between one another is alive with feeling and humming with possibility.

Sometimes the smallest sentiments convey the most joy. . .

"Stay here."

"Come with me."

"Yes."

The golden rule of being joyful

Smile – every time you pass someone.

Yes. Every single time.

Five life moments of sheer unadulterated joy

1. The ecstasy of finally getting your orthodontic braces removed.

2. The explosion of cuteness that ripples through the house when the new puppy comes home.

3. Cheering at the final bell of the summer term.

4. Christmas morning... every year!

5. The pure happiness of holding a newborn baby for the first time.

Everyday joys. . .

Morning snuggles.

Breakfast in bed.

A massage, just because.

An early night.

Starting all over again.

Seven days of joyful living

1. That first day of the holiday.

2. When you notice the cherry blossoms blooming.

3. When the tax deadline passes and you know your form is filed.

4. When you leave the house without a coat on, on the first springlike day of the year.

5. The first snowfall of winter.

6. Christmas Day, when all your loved ones are safely gathered around you.

7. When you wake up and realize you have time for five more minutes...

The joy of small victories...

Actually having the right type of batteries in the cupboard.

Speaking to a real – and helpful – customer services advisor.

Putting in the USB stick the right way round first time.

When the coffee loyalty card pays out and you finally get your free cappuccino.

Joy is seen in the faces of. . .

Family reuniting at airports.

Grandparents holding their grandchild for the first time.

Teachers when their pupil suddenly understands.

Toddlers seeing the sea for the first time.

Cats and dogs when you shake their treat bag.

The joy of. . .

Having a duvet day.

Spending a day without your phone.

Leaving it until tomorrow.

Not going out.

Taking a break.

"A laugh, to be joyous, must flow from a joyous heart, for without kindness, there can be no true joy."

THOMAS CARLYLE

The American Psychological Association defines joy as:

noun

A feeling of extreme gladness, delight, or exultation of the spirit arising from a sense of well-being or satisfaction.

The feeling of joy may take two forms: passive or active.

Passive joy involves tranquility and a feeling of contentment with things as they are.

Active joy involves a desire to share one's joyful feelings with others.

The distinction between passive and active joy may be related to the intensity of the emotion, with active joy being the more intense form. Both forms of joy are associated with an increase in energy and feelings of confidence and positive self-esteem.

dictionary.apa.org

How do you express joy? Do you. . .

Jump for joy?

Dance for joy?

Scream with joy?

Laugh with joy?

Cry with joy?

Or. . .

Do you take yourself away to a quiet
spot and let out a noisy squeal?

**Remember, there is no right or wrong
way to experience joy.**

For three decades, American psychiatrist Professor George Vaillant was the director of the Grant Study, which has been following the lives of 268 men for more than 75 years. It offers extraordinary insights into what makes a life unfurl either with joy or with sadness and difficulty. In a recent article for *The Greater Good* magazine, Professor Vaillant explained that the Grant Study 'finds that nurture trumps nature. And by far the most important influence on a flourishing life is love.'

The way to become a joyful person is by engaging with joyful habits – repeatedly, until those habits are ingrained in our character and we are seen by all those around us as a joyful being.

"Sometimes your joy is the source of your smile, but sometimes your smile can be the source of your joy."

THICH NHAT HANH

Make it a rule to never use your phone when talking to somebody. Try it once and see how levels of joy rise as you both solely concentrate on each other, not on a device.

"There is no beautifier of complexion, or form, or behaviour, like the wish to scatter joy and not pain around us."

RALPH WALDO EMERSON

Make joy your daily intention

Just as you would ask your AI device to 'play happy music', program yourself to get into a joyful mood each morning. Say, 'hey you, let's be intentionally joyful today.' It might take a coffee and a brisk stroll to set the tone, but choosing joy is the first step to feeling it.

Questions to ask yourself at the break of day

1. How can I create joy today?

2. Who shall I bring joy to today?

3. What brings me joy at this very minute?

Questions to ask at the end of the day

1. What brought me joy today?

2. Who shared my joy today?

3. How can I show gratitude for the joy I experienced?

Remember that comparison is the thief of joy

There will always be people with more money, clothes, holidays or pets than you. The trick to maintaining a joyous outlook on life is not to compare yourself to others, and instead to practise showing gratitude for what you already have.

Joy is contagious!

After studying over 4,000 people for 20 years, Harvard professors James H. Fowler and Nicholas A. Christakis observed that happiness can be shared amongst social groups. The study concluded that 'people's happiness depends on the happiness of others with whom they are connected. This provides further justification for seeing happiness, like health, as a collective phenomenon.'

So, the next time you're feeling joyful, don't forget to pass it on!

Craft a joyful personal narrative

Imagine you're meeting yourself for the first time. Think about your introductions and consider whether the story you tell about yourself is truly joyful. Do you say, 'Oh I just look after the children,' or 'I live in a tiny flat but it's all I can afford', or 'My job sucks but it pays the bills'?

While there's no need to lie or even embellish the truth, there are benefits to reframing your story to emphasize the joy it brings you. Try saying: 'I'm so privileged to care for my children full-time,' or, 'I have a cozy flat which is a base for now but I'm planning to move on within the year,' or 'My job? Who cares! What I really love is...'

Shout your joy!

Did someone make you smile? Thank them for making you feel joyful.

When you see an elderly couple walking hand-in-hand, still in love, let them know you've noticed their joy.

When the sun is shining and life is good, tell everyone that today is a joyful day.

If you spend an evening laughing with your friends, remind them that they fill your heart with joy.

Is your mother calling? Before she gets on your case. . . tell her she is a joy.

Feel joy with all five senses

Joy's journey into our hearts begins with the five senses: sight, sound, smell, taste and touch. The luscious view, the song of a nightingale, the scent of your sister's perfume, the taste of devil's food cake or the feel of your cat's plush fur.

Be conscious of the sensory element of joy. Let its effects on the body burn onto your memory so you can revisit them when necessary.

"When you do things from your soul, you feel a river moving in you, a joy."

RUMI

We are surrounded by small moments of joy just waiting to be sensed. Be open to the joy hiding within your ordinary routine.

The first hot sip of coffee.

The unique way your daughter eats her cereal.

The mind-blowing wonder of having a whole world of music available by voice command.

Open your eyes and heart to the lambent joy and wait to be startled into broad smiles.

"*Things won are done; joy's soul lies in the doing.*"

WILLIAM SHAKESPEARE
Troilus and Cressida

Modern floral artist Georgia O'Keeffe spoke wondrously of looking at a flower and the flower becoming the whole world in your hand. Follow her inspiration and seek joy in the small, in the hand held.

Three small ways to feel joy

1. Cup a flower in both hands and spend at least 10 minutes gazing at it. See how the petals unfurl, wonder at the fine veins, breathe in its fragrance.

2. Hold the hand of the person dearest to your heart. Feel their fingers in yours, touch their skin to your mouth, sense the blood pulsing through their veins.

3. Decide not to hold your phone today. Use your hands for picking up a new craft instead.

Joy sounds like. . .

The tune of the ice cream van.

A baby's laugh.

The babble of a brook.

The quiet when the baby sleeps.

Birdsong after the darkest of nights.

Your breath next to mine.

Joy smells like. . .

Candyfloss.

Freshly baked doughnuts.

Pink bubble gum.

Freshly-cut grass.

Children after playing for hours
in the open air.

You, close beside me.

When giving gifts, consider how an abundance of generosity can help generate an extra serving of joy. The exaggerated exuberance brings immediate joy.

Six ideas for joyfully generous gifts

1. A tray of peaches.
2. Nail polishes or lipsticks of entirely different shades.
3. A bouquet of multi-coloured balloons.
4. Multi-coloured socks.
5. A punnet of figs.
6. A window box of herbs.

Treasures to wear to increase joy

Anything silk.

New underwear.

Family jewellery.

The colour you love.

Cashmere thermals.

Flip flops after your first pedicure of the summer.

Like popcorn and chores,
joy is always better shared.

Joy feels like. . .

The nuzzle of a baby in your neck.

Fairies dancing in your stomach.

The warm breath of your loved one.

Electricity coarsing through your
veins.

Discover the Five Minute Rule to allow for joyful encounters

The Five Minute Rule insists that you leave the house five minutes earlier than you need to. These golden five minutes can be reserved for moments of joy – either you arrive early and have five minutes' bliss to yourself to appreciate the scenery, or you have five minutes to indulge in unforeseen encounters. No longer will you have to breathlessly shout, 'Sorry, I've got to dash.' You have five whole extra minutes to have a joyful encounter with whatever – or whomever – fate throws in your path.

Joy is waiting to be practised and experienced, not chased or sought after.

Only 66 days to the more joyful you!

Behavioural scientist James Clear writes that it takes on average two months, or 66 days, for a new habit to become automatic. Why not adopt a new joyful habit today? In 66 days' time, these habits will have evolved into an automatic reflex of joyful behaviour.

"A new life begins for us with every second. Let us go forward joyously to meet it. We must press on, whether we will or no, and we shall walk better with our eyes before us than with them ever cast behind."

JEROME K. JEROME

Joy is not something we receive; it is something we give. Each time we give joy, a little remains in our heart.

Joy is what remains when the fun has stopped, our friends have left and the party has finished. Joy is the residue of good times shared with loved ones.

"He who binds to himself a joy
Does the winged life destroy;
But he who kisses the joy as it flies
Lives in eternity's sunrise."

WILLIAM BLAKE
'Eternity'

Conduct a joy audit

1. Make yourself your favourite drink. Sit in your favourite chair. Open your favourite journal or notebook.

2. Consider each segment of your day, from waking to sleeping.

3. Whenever you encounter joy, be it your morning hot water and lemon or your early evening phone call with your bestie, write down AJ (Appreciate Joy). By consciously labelling these small moments, and actively appreciating them on a regular basis, you will help to illuminate the already joyful aspects of your daily life.

4. Whenever you encounter joyless moments, be it never having freshly ironed shirts or still driving a diesel car, write down FJ (Find Joy). Consider the actions you can take to turn moments of negativity into moments of joy. Plan a time to slot the ironing into your day or begin a savings plan to upgrade to an electric car, for instance. The first step in creating joy is to identify the pinch points in the day and work out what to do about them.

5. Tot up the numbers of AJ vs numbers of FJ.

6. If you have more moments labelled AJ than FJ, give yourself a huge joyful bonus. If your FJ moments outnumber the AJ moments, set yourself a target to even up the numbers by the first quarter – and then for AJ to outstrip FJ by the second quarter.

The first step on the road to joy is gratitude

If joy is the destination, then gratitude is the vehicle.

Practise gratitude: thank the universe for the sun, for your home, for those who love you. Begin with gratitude and joy will follow in its slipstream.

Start a gratitude habit

Every day, write down just one thing you're grateful for. Record these moments in your journal, write them on sticky notes and stick them all over your house, or fill a jar with grateful moments that will bring you joy every time you remember them.

Three questions about joy

1. What makes my heart sing?
2. When did my heart last sing?
3. When will it sing again?

Create a joy mood board

My joyful place is. . .

My joyful people are. . .

My joyful song is. . .

My most joyful food is. . .

My joyful destination is. . .

My joyful view is. . .

My joyful memory is. . .

Be realistic about joy – it's not an emotion we can expect to experience 100% of the time. Think of joy as laughter: wonderful to experience and share with others, but absurd to do all the time.

The joy of. . .

Recovery.

Healing.

The 'all clear'.

Revival.

Reuniting.

Microdose on joy

If the day is beating down on you, microdose on joy. Stop what you're doing for just two minutes. Step outside, turn your face to the sun, read your favourite poem or listen to your favourite piece of music. Remind yourself how it feels to be joyful with one tiny dose, and then return to your day, smiling.

Five microdoses of joy

1. A good stretch.

2. A glass of perfectly chilled champagne.

3. The scent of jasmine.

4. One square of chocolate melting slowly on your tongue.

5. The purr of a kitten.

New Baby!

First day at school!

Bar Mitzvah!

Passed my driving test!

18th birthday party!

We're getting married!

First home!

It is when we connect to what really matters that we shed tears of joy. Consider joyful events – a wedding, a birth, an unexpected but heartfelt gift – as the fairy lights that illuminate your life, each individual glow representing a separate joyful event.

Joy, like all good things, must be nurtured. Joy withers and dies if constantly greeted with negativity and fear. When someone is brimming with joy, has a joyful idea, or wishes to share joyful plans for the future, don't say:

"Oh grow up."

"It won't work."

"Stop messing about."

Do say:

"Great idea!"

"Tell me more."

"How can I help?"

Meet joy with joy

Listen mindfully to how you respond to someone's cheerful mood or online post. So your friend has a new tattoo. It's made her joyful. You think it's horrible. Try your best not to dull someone else's shine: when you attempt to meet joy with joy but don't want to sound insincere, practise straightforward positivity and acceptance: 'I'm so pleased you're happy.'

Practising gratitude helps us to recognize moments of joy in our lives. The next time you say 'thank you', take the gratitude ritual one step further by asking why you are so thankful. If you are grateful for a delicious meal cooked just for you, for example, ask yourself why this moment is particularly meaningful. Understanding the deeper reasons for the pleasure we experience will help us to fully appreciate the joy they bring.

Practise the Taoist meditation of the Inner Smile

1. Find your peaceful place.

2. Sit comfortably.

3. Close your eyes.

4. Wait for the internal chatter to quiet.

5. Pause.

6. Form your Inner Smile. Think of the smile as being as deep as a canyon, as wide as the ocean. Feel the smile reach its arc to the tips of your fingers and the depth of your core.

7. Turn your Inner Smile to each of your organs.

8. Smile to your heart. Fill your heart with your positive energy.

9. Smile to your lungs. Fill your lungs with beams of happiness.

10. Smile to your kidneys. Two nods of deep appreciation.

11. When your body is infused with the joy of your Inner Smile, pause.

12. Return to the moment and continue your day safe in the knowledge that your Inner Smile has already cast joy.

"I learned to look more upon the bright side of my condition, and less upon the dark side, and to consider what I enjoyed rather than what I wanted; and this gave me sometimes such secret comforts, that I cannot express them."

DANIEL DEFOE

A strain of puritanism still runs through western society, leaving in its wake a lingering fear that perhaps, after all, joy might not be a good thing. There is only one answer to this and that's to invite the doom-mongers and the miserable to join you in shaping a joyful and optimistic vision of the present and future.

"I find ecstasy in life; the mere sense of living is joy enough."

EMILY DICKINSON

The joy of being silly

1. Make bananas more joyful by pretending they're a telephone. Have a good conversation with the banana to your ear before eating.

2. Before putting on a pair of socks, attach them to your ears and entertain your loved one with an impression of a spaniel.

3. Cook Friday night supper naked, save a strategically placed apron. Avoid deep frying.

4. Have a big toe kitchen karaoke. This requires one person to sit, sockless, on a kitchen unit. The other person stands and uses the other's big toe as a microphone for joyous kitchen karaoke.

Sometimes joy needs to be speedily ushered in. If a sparkle of joy needs to be sprinkled on proceedings, be that person with the joy-filled handbag ready to get the party started. Distribute the items below with generous abandon and watch as everyone's spirits soar.

1. Glitter.

2. Confetti.

3. Red lipstick.

4. Mobile disco ball.

5. Mini speakers.

While joy is often sudden, loud and seen by all, remember to nurture quiet moments of joy, too. Be vigilant about creating space and silence in your daily routine so your mind and body are able to expand and relax. Time without plans is not empty – it is in fact space waiting to be filled with what will bring you the most joy.

Things to wear to increase joy

Yellow.

Polka dots.

A jaunty scarf around your neck.

A beret.

Red shoes.

Invest in a pair of red dungarees.
For some mysterious reason, red
dungarees never fail to make the
wearer feel anything less than joyful.
Save them for a joyful dungaree day
and wear them with a skip in your step.

Three ways to colour yourself joyful!

Decorate every nail and toenail a different colour.

Rethread your shoes with colourful new laces.

Wear flowers in your hair.

Jot down joy

Joy is everywhere – in the early morning birdsong and in the clasped hands of the elderly couple walking along the seafront. Get into the habit of jotting down joy on your phone or in your journal. Keep the list open and see how swiftly it grows. On dull days that need a lift, refer to your joy jottings and relive those happy moments.

Three ways to make space for joy

1. Work out how much time you spend on your phone. If the majority of your screentime is mindless scrolling, leave the phone at home and honour yourself with a joyful experience instead.

2. Schedule in an empty hour every day. Plan nothing. When the hour arrives, listen to yourself. What would bring you joy, right here and right now? A run? A hair wash? To cook a feast? Fulfil your joyful wish.

3. Remove one thing from your daily schedule. Thin out your commitments – especially anything you don't truly love – to create more time for spontaneous joy.

Don't be embarrassed by joy. Be bold! Once you've made space for joy, make sure to fill the space with anything and everything that makes you happy.

LOVE.

FAMILY.

RELIGION.

TRIATHLONS.

OPERA.

ONLINE GAMING.

MIXED MARTIAL ARTS.

LEARNING THE FLUTE.

Whatever makes your heart sing.

Actively create a desirable place in which to be joyful

Imagine yourself as a figure in a glorious landscape painting and ask yourself how you can spark joy in your own environment. Could you tidy up, redecorate, even move neighbourhoods? Create surroundings that burst with joy – and bask in the joy they bequeath you.

Create outer order to feel inner joy

Tidy the pile of stuff on the table.

Put the car through the wash.

Invest in under-the-bed storage boxes.

Take time to appreciate the clear surface, shiny car and ordered bedroom.

Smile as joy reigns in the absence of chaos and disorder.

Six easy ways to inject joy into mundane tasks

1. Invest in snazzy kitchen equipment: feathered washing up gloves, knives with leopard skin handles or multi-coloured spoons and stirrers.

2. Always use more bubbles than are needed: go heavy on the washing up liquid so there's always the potential to dab a pawful on the nose of your nearest and dearest.

3. Pump up the volume: kitchen discos are not just for parties! Why not have one every time you unload the dishwasher?

4. Chuck it all out: Fed up with dusting the shelf of clutter? Have a yard sale and reduce, reduce, reduce!

5. Sing until the job is done: when embarking on your least favourite task – such as cleaning the loo – sing your favourite song at the top of your lungs and don't stop until the job is done. Come to a rousing crescendo finale with the final chorus as you slam down the now-gleaming lid of the toilet.

6. Stick googly eyes to the scrubbing brush, toilet brush and the vegetable peeler. Turning inanimate objects into silly cartoon characters will make even the most mundane tasks more joyful.

Embrace the German concept of *Die Geborgenheit*

Germans have a suitably complicated but charming word to explain the joy that comes from security. Die Geborgenheit isn't easily translated into English but it describes the profound sense of warmth felt when in a place of safety, security and comfort. Die Geborgenheit refers not merely to your surroundings but the peaceful sense of contentment you feel in yourself.

"A thing of beauty is a joy forever:
Its loveliness increases; it will never
Pass into nothingness; but still will keep
A bower quiet for us, and a sleep
Full of sweet dreams, and health, and
quiet breathing."

JOHN KEATS
from 'Endymion'

Joy is hard to find in a muddle. If the flat is too messy, the journey to work too rushed or the to-do list too long, joy will remain elusive.

Stop. Think. Plan.

Write a cleaning roster, set the alarm 10 minutes earlier, say no to a few commitments. This may be dreary advice, but it works for long-term joy. Clear the decks and make space for joy to enter your schedule.

Appreciate your joyful 'things of beauty'

Thanks to Marie Kondo, we all know that objects and clothes are not merely lifeless, but can instead magnificently 'spark joy'.

Think of yourself as a museum curator and carefully elevate your favourite pieces that 'spark joy.'

Spark joy, Marie Kondo-style

Does your favourite print or painting need reframing? Could your grandma's brooch be worn more often? Those crystal glasses that you've been saving for a special occasion – how about using them this weekend?

Discover JOMO: the Joy of Missing Out

JOMO was coined by Christina Cook, 'Chief Joy Officer' and founder of ExperienceJOMO.com. It's all about making the most of those moments when plans fall through, turning the notion of FOMO (the Fear of Missing Out) on its head.

Sometimes, there is nothing quite so pleasurable as a cancelled invitation. Rather than feeling disappointed about missing an engagement, seize the opportunity for yourself: take that bath you've been longing for, call up an old friend for a long chat, finish the project that's been niggling at you. Or merely do nothing. Pause. Reset.

JOMO is the art of living a smaller life, better

Full acknowledgement of your true priorities – and sticking to them without bending to external pressure – is at the heart of the JOMO movement. So, if you would rather spend time at home with your family, do so. If you don't want a digital presence, don't have one. If your horizons are narrow, so be it; contribute to a caring community at home.

The reward of JOMO is strengthened relationships and the shoring up of community bonds.

The JOMO movement is all about reclaiming self-determined joy: choosing how to spend your time and energy, rather than falling in with what society demands of you.

JOMO makes you happy to:

Say no.

Live life offline.

Develop fewer, better relationships.

Joy tastes like. . .

Homemade lemonade in the sunshine.

Anything your child bakes.

Thirst quenching water.

Tea, biscuits and a chat.

Steaming soul food on a cold night.

If you fill your life with joy there will inevitably be less space to pack with melancholy and despair. Think of joy as a bodily barrier to negativity.

*"Joy takes a strange effect at times,
it seems to oppress us almost the same
as sorrow."*

ALEXANDRE DUMAS
The Count of Monte Cristo

Host a joyful dinner party

1. Invite all those closest to you who bring you joy.

2. Set a cracker down at each place – why should this particular joy be reserved only for Christmas?

3. Cook, serve or order in the food that brings you joy.

4. Write a note for each of your dining companions explaining how they have brought you joy. Place a note in each glass and ask your guests to read theirs aloud before filling the glass with your joyful drink of choice.

5. Raise a 'toast to joy'. In the words of 17th century poet John Dryden, here's to 'Merry, dancing, drinking, laughing, quaffing, and unthinking time'!

6. Tuck in and let the joyful festivities begin!

Recipe for family joy

Ingredients:

1 cup fun

2 cups patience

½ cup honesty

20 cups love

Method:

Mix together and serve up on a daily basis.

Tip:

If it doesn't work out, simply try again with an extra cup of love.

"I slept and dreamt that life was joy.
I awoke and saw that life was service.
I acted and behold, service was joy."

RABINDRANATH TAGORE

"If there ever was a pursuit which stultified itself by its very conditions, it is the pursuit of pleasure as the all-sufficing end of life. Happiness cannot come to any man capable of enjoying true happiness unless it comes as the sequel to duty well and honestly done."

THEODORE ROOSEVELT

"Those who do not know the torment of the unknown cannot have the joy of discovery which is certainly the liveliest that the mind of man can ever feel."

CLAUDE BERNARD

The French philosopher Descartes decided that *la béatitude* (happiness) was inevitable for those who act virtuously. He wrote that 'we cannot ever practise any virtue – that is to say, do what our reason tells us we should do – without receiving satisfaction and pleasure from doing so'.

So what are the virtues we should engage in that will bring us joy? Descartes is not prescriptive, but rather explains that all the usual virtues such as justice, courage, temperance, develop from a 'firm and powerful resolve always to use [one's] reasoning powers correctly, as far as he can, and to carry out whatever he knows to be best'.

In other words... if we follow our conscience and behave as we know we should – treating people kindly and fairly – joy will inevitably follow.

" *It seems that the difference between the greatest souls and those that are base and common consists principally in the fact that common souls abandon themselves to their passions and are happy or unhappy only according as the things that happen to them are agreeable or unpleasant; the greatest souls, on the other hand, reason in a way that is so strong and cogent that,*

*although they also have passions,
and indeed passions which are often
more violent than those of ordinary
people, their reason nevertheless
always remains mistress, and even
makes their afflictions serve them and
contribute to the perfect happiness
they enjoy in this life.*"

DESCARTES
in letters to Princess Elisabeth of Bohemia

For the Stoics, joy is not a frivolous matter; rather, its attainment requires a rather stern approach to pleasure. Seneca's classic Stoic essay *On the Happy Life* was addressed to his brother Gallio when Seneca was 62. He begins, 'All men, brother Gallio, wish to live happily, but are dull at perceiving exactly what it is that makes life happy.' Seneca further unpacks this idea, explaining that men achieve joyful living when they live virtuously, striking a balance between pleasures of the flesh and pleasures of the mind. By using reason and moderation, happiness and joy become a delightful bonus.

" *Pleasure is not the reward or the cause of virtue, but comes in addition to it; nor do we choose virtue because she gives us pleasure, but she gives us pleasure also if we choose her.*"

On the Happy Life

"Know the joy of life by piling good deed on good deed until no rift or cranny appears between them."

MARCUS AURELIUS

There is something celestial about the experience of joy. It can be found shining brightly in the space between people and their divine beliefs – be that a religious deity or simply a deep appreciation for the arts. Such a joyous connection causes sparks to fly between people, leaving embers burning forever within their hearts.

"Be moderate in order to taste the joys of life in abundance."

EPICURUS

For millennia, joy has been bound up with the experience of the divine. Whether through a personal religious experience or through cultural religious rituals that have been passed down to us, the experience of joy when contemplating a deity is felt globally and universally.

"The Lord is one life shining forth from every creature. Seeing him present in all, the wise man is humble, puts not himself forward. His delight is in the Self, His joy is in the Self, he serves the Lord in all."

Mundaka Upanishad

"So I commend the enjoyment of life, because there is nothing better for a person under the sun than to eat and drink and be glad. Then joy will accompany them in their toil all the days of the life God has given them under the sun."

Ecclesiastes 8:15

"True happiness is to rejoice in the truth, for to rejoice in the truth is to rejoice in You, O God, who are the Truth."

ST AUGUSTINE

"When you feel a peaceful joy, that's when you are near the truth."

RUMI

Joy is not exclusive. There is a commonality to joy for it is waiting for us in the natural world. We are all capable of experiencing joy in the physical world around us.

"Every season is likeable, and wet days and fine, red wine and white, company and solitude. Even sleep, that deplorable curtailment of the joy of life, can be full of dreams; and the most common actions – a walk, a talk, solitude in one's own orchard – can be enhanced and lit up by the association of the mind. Beauty is everywhere, and beauty is only two finger's-breadth from goodness."

VIRGINIA WOOLF

Joy is invigorating. Joy can be found in the extremes of experience, those exhilarating moments when we reach the mountain's summit or dive into white horse waves. Consider the wild, far flung elements that nature offers and embrace its spine tingling joy.

" We can never have enough of Nature. We must be refreshed by the sight of inexhaustible vigour, vast and titanic features, the sea-coast with its wrecks, the wilderness with its living and its decaying trees, the thunder-cloud, and the rain which last three weeks and produces freshets."

HENRY DAVID THOREAU

Joy can be most vividly experienced when a connection is made between two people and the natural world that surrounds them: when extreme beauty touches humanity.

Three ways to seek joy in nature

1. Watching a sunset with your lover.

2. Swimming in the sea with your children.

3. Forest bathing with your bestie.

Find joy in one place

1. Choose a spot in your garden, street or a nearby park where you feel uplifted.

2. Agree to spend a few moments in the same spot once a week.

3. When you're in your joyful place, open up your senses and let the joy flood you. Feel the weather on your face, heed the noises all around, breathe deeply and let your nostrils twitch at the scent on the breeze.

4. Consider bringing a notebook, a camera, or tape recorder. When moved by the changing majesty of your joyful spot, record it or write it down.

5. As time and seasons unfurl, pay careful attention to how your joyful place embraces these changes. See the leaves dance in the autumn wind, watch as the frost crisps around spring buds and marvel as the clouds skim past.

6. With repeated visits, the images and sensations of your joyful place will seer on your memory, allowing you to draw on its sense of beauty whenever you require.

The thrill of joy lies in the sense that, by experiencing it, we are vitally alive and living at the very outer edges of human capacity. Like the wild abandon and shout of laughter when leaping into a swimming pool, joy as experienced in nature is a powerful reminder that we are alive and kicking.

In 2010, the *Journal of Environmental Psychology* reported that being outdoors was associated with feelings of greater vitality – the joyous feeling of vigour and energy. Nature-fed vitality gives the hiker/mountaineer/woodland walker uplifting energy that can be utilized for positive purposes.

"Climb the mountains and get their good tidings. Nature's peace will flow into you as sunshine flows into trees. The winds will blow their own freshness into you, and the storms their energy, while cares will drop off like autumn leaves."

JOHN MUIR

Even when you're not feeling joyful, keep your senses attuned to all the expressions of joy happening around you. The sun will keep shining and the glory of the natural world will continue to wait for you to behold its splendours.

Listen out for joy

Sit outside, or by an open window if it's too chilly. Close your eyes and listen for a short time. Perhaps set an alarm for five minutes. Listen mindfully and you might catch the trill of a songbird, or the trundle of a child's scooter. Listen for the rustle of the wind or the soft fall of rain. Afterwards, jot down what you heard and how it made you feel. If prose is not your thing, sketch, write a poem or send a message to a friend, sharing the delightful sounds you discovered with them.

If this brought you joy, do it again tomorrow – there's no limit on the amount of joy we can allow ourselves.

Five ways to find joy in nature

1. Adopt a dog. Not only will the dog bring you joy, but taking your pooch for an outdoor walk will let you bask in the joy of nature every day.

2. Listen to yourself and discover what YOU love: wild water swimming is not everyone's idea of joy, but sunbathing on a roof terrace may be more your thing. Experiment with which areas of the natural world bring you pleasure – and allow yourself to indulge.

3. Walk with children: if the cold outside has lost its sparkling allure, take young cousins, nieces or nephews with you to rediscover the joy with which they approach everything from crunchy leaves to dead logs, puddles and ponds.

4. Grow something: it can be joyous to watch cress grow on a damp towel or herbs erupt with life.

5. Open the window: if life tethers you indoors, welcome the outdoors in.

Joy is for everyone – not only those cheerful animated types.

Joy felt within your heart is the seed;
your heart's joy shared is the flower.

"A flower blossoms for its own joy. We gain a moment of joy by looking at it."

OSCAR WILDE

"Joy's smile is much closer to tears than to laughter."

VICTOR HUGO

"It is a fair, even-handed, noble adjustment of things, that while there is infection in disease and sorrow, there is nothing in the world so irresistibly contagious as laughter and good-humour."

CHARLES DICKENS

"Honest good-humour is the oil and wine of a merry meeting, and there is no jovial companionship equal to that where the jokes are rather small and laughter abundant."

WASHINGTON IRVING

Jupiter, sometimes called Jove, was the Roman king of the Gods – their version of Zeus. The largest of the planets, Jupiter, is named after him. According to astrology, those born under the planet Jupiter are blessed with all the good things: power, wealth, success and, most importantly, joy and happiness. The word jovial (from Jove) is used to describe anyone born with a good nature and cheerful spirit.

When Gustav Holst, the Victorian composer, wrote his orchestral suite 'The Planets', his movement for Jupiter was called: 'Jupiter, the Bringer of Jollity'.

Play it loud and fill yourself with planetary joy.

The Ancient Greeks believed pearls were the tears of joy shed by the Goddess Aphrodite. Wear a string of pearls around your neck or dangle a pair of pearl earrings from your ears to signify joy.

Choose Matisse's 'Bonheur de Vivre' as your screensaver

Daubed in vivid yellows, blues and pinks, Henri Matisse's painting 'Bonheur de Vivre' ('The Joy of Life') is a joyful expression of all that is fabulous about life. Nearly two and a half metres wide, the exuberant canvas depicts naked men and women dancing, making music and engaging in languid erotic acts. It is a scene of halcyon bliss. First exhibited in 1906, it was described by some critics as 'disgusting', but it has come to be regarded as a formative work of the modernist art scene. The 'Bonheur de Vivre' now hangs in The Barnes Foundation, Philadelphia – and it makes a fantastic laptop screensaver.

According to *Classic FM* magazine, 'Joy to the World' was America's most published Christmas hymn in the late 20th century.

"*Joy to the world! the Lord is come;*
Let earth receive her King;
Let every heart prepare him room,
And heaven and nature sing,
And heaven and nature sing,
And heaven, and heaven, and nature
sing.
Joy to the world! the Saviour reigns;
Let men their songs employ;
While fields and floods, rocks, hills, and
plains
Repeat the sounding joy,
Repeat the sounding joy,
Repeat, repeat the sounding joy."

ISAAC WATTS
from 'Joy to the World'

Just 30ml of Joy, the perfume created by Henri Alméras in 1929, requires 10,000 jasmine flowers and twenty-eight dozen roses. The iconic scent was created just after the Wall Street Crash for Parisian couterier Jean Patou; the heady fragrance was an instant success and it was voted 'Fragrance of the Century' in 2000 at the Fragrance Foundation FiFi Awards. Take inspiration from Alméras and douse yourself in your favourite fragrance for an instant hit of joy.

Jump for Joy was a pioneering musical revue written by Duke Ellington. It stared an all-African American cast and ran for 122 performances in Los Angeles in 1941. Ellington's song 'Jump for Joy' tackled racial issues and included thought-provoking lyrics to make the audience think.

Four haikus about joy

Joy is your own choice
Yours to make, yours to create
Feel joy around you.

As the sun beats down
Joy emerges unbroken.
Step out from the shade

Joy is a heartbeat:
Fueling the body with life,
Feel it while you can

The sparrow flew low;
when joy caught its feathered breast.
Now it soars above.

Write your own joyful haiku

The next time the joyful mood takes you, try penning your own haiku.

This Japanese poetry form is made up of three lines of five, seven, and then five syllables. Being so short, you can scribble down a new haiku on anything from a sticky note to a napkin – the perfect snapshot of joy from a fun day.

"On with the dance! 'Let joy be unconfined' is my motto, whether there's any dance to dance; or any joy to unconfine."

MARK TWAIN

A 2011 study by the University of Groningen in the Netherlands showed that listening to happy music can affect people's perception of the world. Joyful songs in the major key, with 150 beats per minute and positive lyrics, make people feel happy and view the world more positively.

"*Surprised by joy — impatient as the Wind*
I turned to share the transport - Oh! with whom
But Thee, long buried in the silent tomb,
That spot which no vicissitude can find?
Love, faithful love, recalled thee to my mind -
But how could I forget thee? - Through what power,
Even for the least division of an hour,
Have I been so beguiled as to be blind
To my most grievous loss? - That thought's return

Was the worst pang that sorrow ever bore,
Save one, one only, when I stood forlorn,
Knowing my heart's best treasure was no more;
That neither present time, nor years unborn
Could to my sight that heavenly face restore."

WILLIAM WORDSWORTH
'Surprised by Joy'

"Joy, beautiful spark of Divinity,
Daughter of Elysium,
We enter, drunk with fire,
Heavenly one, thy sanctuary!
Thy magic binds again
What custom strictly divided;
All people become brothers,
Where thy gentle wing abides."

FRIEDRICH SCHILLER
from 'Ode to Joy'

'Ode to Joy', originally titled 'An die Freude', is the tub-thumping poem written in 1785 by German polymath Friedrich Schiller about the universal brotherhood created by war and desperation. Famously set to music by Ludwig van Beethoven, the tune (but not Schiller's words) is currently used as the anthem of the European Union.

Five joyful classical pieces

1. 'Gloria', Vivaldi.

2. 'The Nutcracker Suite', Tchaikovsky.

3. 'Volière from 'Carnival of the Animals', Camille Saint-Saëns.

4. 'Symphony No. 1', Prokofiev.

5. 'Piano Sonata in G minor', Clara Schumann.

Five joyful pop songs

1. 'Good Vibrations', The Beach Boys.

2. 'Happy', Pharrell Williams.

3. 'I got you (I feel good)', James Brown.

4. 'Twist and Shout', The Beatles.

5. 'Walking on Sunshine', Katrina & The Waves.

The joy of. . .

Well-fitting clothes.

A five star Uber rating.

The pop of the cork.

A hand-written thank you letter.

Freshly laundered white shirts.

whowhatwear.co.uk listed five fashion brands that have made the most joyful catwalk looks. Think tulle, tutus, intense colour, sequins, neon, and clothes to make you sing with joy.

1. Christopher John Rogers.

2. Shrimps.

3. Molly Goddard.

4. Ganni.

5. Halpern.

" Long live the sun which gives us such beautiful colour."

PAUL CÉZANNE

" *Both were so young, and one so innocent,*
That bathing pass'd for nothing; Juan seem'd
To her, as 'twere, the kind of being sent,
Of whom these two years she had nightly dream'd,
A something to be loved, a creature meant
To be her happiness, and whom she deem'd
To render happy; all who joy would win
Must share it, – Happiness was born a twin."

LORD BYRON,
from 'Don Juan' (Canto II)

Victorian society was gripped by floriography, the language of flowers. In 1884, Kate Greenaway, a star illustrator, printed *The Language of Flowers*, a sumptuously illustrated reference book where all emotions and meanings were listed with their corresponding flower. The flowers listed here represent joy in its many forms.

- American starwort: cheerfulness in old age.

- Butterfly orchid: gaiety.

- Celandine (lesser): joys to come.

- Coreopsis: always cheerful.

- Everlasting sweet pea: lasting pleasure.

- Mugwort: happiness.

- Myrrh: gladness.

- White periwinkle: pleasures of memory.

- Wood sorrel: joy.

- Xeranthemum: cheerfulness under adversity.

- Volkamenia: may you be happy.

- White mullein: good nature.

"The joy of life is variety; the tenderest love requires to be rekindled by intervals of absence."

SAMUEL JOHNSON

"People are constantly clamouring for the joy of life. As for me, I find the joy of life in the hard and cruel battle of life – to learn something is a joy to me."

AUGUST STRINDBERG

"There is something terribly morbid in the modern sympathy with pain. One should sympathize with the colour, the beauty, the joy of life. The less said about life's sores the better."

OSCAR WILDE

"The sweetest joys of life grow in the very jaws of its perils."

HERMAN MELVILLE

"*Elinor could sit still no longer. She almost ran out of the room, and as soon as the door was closed, burst into tears of joy, which at first she thought would never cease.*"

JANE AUSTEN
Sense and Sensibility

"'Take some books and read; that's an immense help; books are always good company if you have the right sort. Let me pick out some for you.' And Mrs. Jo made a bee-line to the well-laden shelves, which were the joy of her heart and the comfort of her life."

LOUISA MAY ALCOTT
Jo's Boys

"Oh, frabjous day! Callooh. Callay!
He chortled in his joy."

LEWIS CARROLL
from 'Jabberwocky'

"Give me a moment, because I like to cry for joy. It's so delicious, John dear, to cry for joy."

CHARLES DICKENS
Our Mutual Friend

Cherish those people who have known you all your life. There is a joyous distinction to folk who have known and loved you since babyhood. Often marked by an effortless sense of loving familiarity, these lifelong relationships are impossible to recreate. Recognize the joy in longevity.

*"Down the dimpled green-sward
dancing
Bursts a flaxen-headed bevy,
Bud-lipt boys and girls advancing
Love's irregular little levy.*

*Rows of liquid eyes in laughter,
How they glimmer, how they quiver!
Sparkling one another after,
Like bright ripples on a river.*

*Tipsy band of rubious faces,
Flushed with joy's etheral spirit,
Make your mocks and sly grimaces
At Love's self, and do not fear it!"*

GEORGE DARLEY
'The Joy Of Childhood'

Joy is always a possibility

Even if you are walking through the shadow of devastating loss, there is still the potential to experience joy again. While you may not be ready to seek out new joyous experiences, you can choose to remember gentle, joyful memories – a choice that can be tenderly made amidst crushing grief.

"Remember me with smiles and laughter, for that is how I will remember you all. If you can only remember me with tears, then don't remember me at all."

LAURA INGALLS WILDER

"There have been times when I have fallen asleep in tears; but in my dreams the most charming forms have come to console and cheer me, and I have risen fresh and joyful."

JOHANN WOLFGANG VON GOETHE

" The pain was short –
eternal joy succeeds."

FRIEDRICH SCHILLER

QUOTES ARE TAKEN FROM

Alexandre Dumas, 1802–1870, French novelist and playwright

August Strindberg, 1849–1912, Swedish playwright, author, poet and painter

Charles Dickens, 1812–1870, English author and social critic

Claude Bernard, 1813–1878, French physiologist

Daniel Defoe, 1660–1731, English writer, journalist and pamphleteer

Descartes, 1596–1650, French philosopher, mathematician and scientist

Eleonora Duse, 18658–1924, Italian actress

Emily Dickinson, 1830–1886, American poet

Epicurus, 341BC–270BC, ancient Greek philosopher and sage

Friedrich Schiller, 1759–1805, German playwright, poet and philosopher

George Darley, 1795–1846, Irish poet, novelist and literary critic

Henry David Thoreau, 1817–1862 American naturalist

Herman Melville, 1819–1891, American writer

Isaac Watts, 1674–1748, English hymn writer, theologian and logician

Jane Austen, 1775–1817, English novelist

Jerome K. Jerome, 1859–1927, English writer and humourist

Johann Wolfgang von Goethe, 1749–1832, German polymath

John Keats, 1795–1821, English Romantic poet

John Muir, 1838–1914, Scottish-American naturalist and advocate for the preservation of American wildernesses

Laura Ingalls Wilder, 1867–1957, American writer

Lewis Carroll, 1832–1898, English writer, illustrator and teacher

Lord Byron, 1788–1824, English Romantic poet

Louisa May Alcott, 1832–1888, American writer

Marcus Aurelius, 121AD–180AD, Roman emperor and Stoic philosopher

Mark Twain, 1835–1910, American writer, publisher and lecturer

Oscar Wilde, 1854–1900, Irish writer

Paul Cézanne, 1839–1906, French artist

Rabindranath Tagore, 1861–1941, Bengali polymath and writer

Ralph Waldo Emerson, 1803–1882, American essayist and abolitionist

Rumi, 1207–1273, Persian poet

Seneca, c. 4BC– 65AD, Roman Stoic philosopher and dramatist

Samuel Johnson, 1709–1784, English writer, editor and lexicographer

St Augustine, 354AD–430AD, theologian and philosopher

Theodore Roosevelt, 1858–1919, 26th American President

Thich Nhat Hanh, 1926–2022, Thai monk

Thomas Carlyle, 1795–1881, Scottish historian, philosopher, translator and writer

Victor Hugo, 1802–1885, French writer

Virginia Woolf, 1882–1941, English writer

Washington Irving, 1783–1859, American writer and diplomat

William Blake, 1757–1827, English Romantic poet

William Wordsworth, 1770–1850, English Romantic poet

William Shakespeare, 1564–1616, English playwright and poet

Zoroaster, Ancient Persian prophet

JOYFUL READING LIST

Atomic Habits, James Clear, Random House Business, 2018

Happiness – Essential Mindfulness Practices, Thich Nhat Hanh, Parallax Press, 2009

Joyful, Ingrid Fetell Lee, Rider, 2021

The Happiness Project, Gretchen Rubin, HarperCollins, 2012

The Little Book of Lykke, Meik Wiking, Penguin, 2018

The Unexpected Joy of the Ordinary, Catherine Gray, Aster, 2019

SCHOLARLY ARTICLES CITED

Jolij, J., Meurs, M., (2011), 'Music Alters Visual Perception', *PLoS ONE* 6(4).
DOI: 10.1371/journal.pone.0018861

Fowler, J. H., Christakis, N. A. (2008), 'Dynamic spread of happiness in a large social network: longitudinal analysis over 20 years in the Framingham Heart Study', *BMJ* 337.
DOI: 10.1136/bmj.a2338

Vaillant, G. E., McArthur, C. C.; Bock, A. (2022), 'Grant Study of Adult Development, 1938-2000', *Harvard Dataverse* V4. DOI: 10.7910/DVN/48WRX9,

JOYFUL WEBSITES

academyofideas.com

aestheticsofjoy.com

archive.org

experiencejomo.com

forbes.com

happier.com

konmari.com

Managing Director Sarah Lavelle
Assistant Editor Sofie Shearman
Words Joanna Gray
Series Designer Emily Lapworth
Designer Alicia House
Proofreader Lauren Voaden
Head of Production Stephen Lang
Production Controller Sabeena Atchia

Published in 2022 by Quadrille,
an imprint of Hardie Grant
Publishing

Quadrille
52–54 Southwark Street
London SE1 1UN
quadrille.com

The publisher has made every
effort to trace the copyright
holders. We apologize in advance
for any unintentional omissions
and would be pleased to insert the
appropriate acknowledgement in
any subsequent edition.

Cataloguing in Publication Data:
a catalogue record for this book is
available from the British Library.

ISBN 978 1 78713 804 9

Printed in China